HAL•LEONARD

JAZZ PLAY-ALONG®

Book and CDs for B♭, E♭, C and Bass Clef Instruments

volume 1A

Maiden Voyage
ALL BLUES
15 Easy-to-Play Jazz Songs

G000293244

Arranged and Produced by Mark Taylor and Jim Roberts

BOOK

TITLE	PAGE NUMBERS			
	C Treble Instruments	B♭ Instruments	E♭ Instruments	C Bass Instruments
All Blues	8	26	44	62
Autumn Leaves	10	28	46	64
Doxy	9	27	45	63
Footprints	12	30	48	66
Freddie Freeloader	13	31	49	67
How Insensitive (Insensatez)	14	32	50	68
Impressions	16	34	52	70
Little Sunflower	17	35	53	71
Maiden Voyage	18	36	54	72
Now's the Time	19	37	55	73
Recorda-Me	20	38	56	74
Satin Doll	22	40	58	76
Solar	21	39	57	75
Song for My Father	24	42	60	78
Yesterdays	25	43	61	79

ISBN 978-1-4234-7099-1

HAL•LEONARD® CORPORATION

7777 W. BLUEMOUND RD. P.O. BOX 13819 MILWAUKEE, WI 53213

Visit Hal Leonard Online at
www.halleonard.com

Maiden Voyage
ALL BLUES

CDs

TITLE	CD Track Number Split Track/Melody	CD Track Number Full Stereo Track
CD1		
All Blues	1	2
Autumn Leaves	3	4
Doxy	5	6
Footprints	7	8
Freddie Freeloader	9	10
How Insensitive (Insensatez)	11	12
Impressions	13	14
Little Sunflower	15	16
B♭ Tuning Notes		17
CD2		
Maiden Voyage	1	2
Now's the Time	3	4
Recorda-Me	5	6
Satin Doll	7	8
Solar	9	10
Song for My Father	11	12
Yesterdays	13	14
B♭ Tuning Notes		15

MAIDEN VOYAGE/ALL BLUES

Volume 1A

Arranged and Produced by
Mark Taylor and Jim Roberts

Featured Players:

Graham Breedlove–Trumpet and Fluglehorn
John Desalme–Tenor Saxophone
Tony Nalker–Piano
Jim Roberts–Bass
Todd Harrison–Drums
Steve Fidyk–Drums

Recorded at Bias Studios, Springfield, Virginia
Bob Dawson, Engineer

HOW TO USE THE CD:

Each song has <u>two</u> tracks:

1) Split Track/Melody

Woodwind, Brass, Keyboard, and **Mallet Players** can use this track as a learning tool for melody style and inflection.

Bass Players can learn and perform with this track – remove the recorded bass track by turning down the volume on the LEFT channel.

Keyboard and **Guitar Players** can learn and perform with this track – remove the recorded piano part by turning down the volume on the RIGHT channel.

2) Full Stereo Track

Soloists or **Groups** can learn and perform with this accompaniment track with the RHYTHM SECTION only.

SCALES

A scale is a sequentially organized group of notes that begin and end on a specific note. In Western music, the chromatic scale represents all the possible notes between a note and its octave. For example, here is the chromatic scale starting on C:

C C#/D♭ D D#/E♭ E F F#/G♭ A A#/B♭ B C

The major scale is the foundation of Western music—melodies and harmonies are derived from it. To create any major scale we follow a specific pattern of half steps and whole steps. A half step is the distance from a note to the very next note. For example, C to C#/D♭ is a half step. A whole step is two half steps in a row, for example C to D. The pattern for any major scale is:

W	W	H	W	W	W	H
Whole	Whole	Half	Whole	Whole	Whole	Half

In the key of C this is:

C	D	E	F	G	A	B	C
1	2	3	4	5	6	7	8 (1)

A very practical way of looking at scales is to think in terms of scale formulas. In any major scale, the starting note or root is referred to as 1, the second note is referred to as 2, and so on. When you reach the octave of the root it is number 8 but can also be thought of as 1 starting over.

MODES

Modes are similar to scales and are also a sequentially organized group of notes that begin and end on a specific note. However, modes are created by starting and ending on any one of the notes other than the root of a parent scale like the major, melodic minor, harmonic minor, and harmonic major scales. Because there are seven notes in each of those scales, there are seven different modes contained within each scale. For example, if we played the notes of a C major scale starting and ending on D, this series of notes is referred to as the D Dorian mode.

C Major		C	D	E	F	G	A	B	C	
D Dorian			D	E	F	G	A	B	C	D

While both C major and D Dorian share the same notes, the difference is that one scale revolves around a C tonal center and the other revolves around a D tonal center. This means that every note in the scale has a different pull against its respective root. For example, if we played the note F against C, it would sound unresolved, while against D, the note sounds perfectly stable.

All modes can be thought of in terms of scale formulas, in relation to a major scale with the same root. For example, the scale formula for the Dorian mode is: 1–2–♭3–4–5–6–♭7–8.

SCALE SYLLABUS
Using the Scale Syllabus

A good approach would be to first learn and spend a lot of time with the following scales and modes:

> Major (Ionian) and Lydian for major chords
>
> Dorian and Melodic Minor for minor chords
>
> Mixolydian for dominant chords
>
> Locrian for minor7♭5 chords

These scales will cover the majority of your basic needs when playing over jazz standards. You can add other scales to your repertoire as the need arises. For example, learn the diminished half/whole scale when you come across a tune with a 13♭9 chord.

Don't get so hung up on trying to memorize a ton of scales. In the beginning there's some kind of mystique about learning all of these exotic-sounding scales. Keep in mind that even with the complicated-sounding names of some of the scales you'll come across, most often they are just a scale you already know with one or more notes changed. And no great jazz player has exclusively used scales in a solo. Most great solos combine various elements and techniques.

Fundamental Scales and Modes

NAME	FORMULA	TONIC CHORD	COMMON DIATONIC EXTENSIONS
MAJOR			
Major Pentatonic	1 2 3 5 6	6	9
Major (Ionian)	1 2 3 4 5 6 7	maj7	9, 13
Bebop Major	1 2 3 4 5 ♯5 6 7	maj7	9, 13
Lydian	1 2 3 ♯4 5 6 7	maj7	9, ♯11, 13
Lydian ♯2	1 ♯2 3 ♯4 5 6 7	maj7	♯9, ♯11, 13
Lydian Augmented	1 2 3 ♯4 ♯5 6 7	maj7♯5	9, ♯11
Augmented	1 ♯2 3 5 ♯5 7	maj7♯5	♯9, 5
DOMINANT			
Mixolydian	1 2 3 4 5 6 ♭7	7 or 7sus4	9, 13
Bebop Dominant	1 2 3 4 5 6 ♭7 7	7	9, 13
Lydian ♭7	1 2 3 ♯4 5 6 ♭7	7	9, ♯11, 13
Whole Tone	1 2 3 ♯4 ♯5 ♭7	7♯5	9, ♯11
Mixolydian ♭6	1 2 3 4 5 ♭6 ♭7	7♯5	9
Diminished half/whole	1 ♭2 ♯2 3 ♯4 5 6 ♭7	7	♭9, ♯9, ♯11, 13
Super Locrian	1 ♭2 ♭3 ♭4 ♭5 ♭6 ♭7	7♭5 or 7♯5	♭9, ♯9, ♯11, ♭13
Phrygian	1 ♭2 3 4 5 ♭6 ♭7	7sus4	♭9, ♯9 (♭3)
Dorian ♭2	1 ♭2 ♭3 4 5 6 ♭7	7sus4	♭9, ♯9 (♭3), 13
MINOR			
Minor Pentatonic	1 ♭3 4 5 ♭7	min7	11
Blues	1 ♭3 4 ♭5 5 ♭7	min7	11
Dorian	1 2 ♭3 4 5 6 ♭7	min7	9, 11, 13
Bebop Minor	1 2 ♭3 4 5 ♯5 6 ♭7	min7	9, 11, 13
Melodic Minor	1 2 ♭3 4 5 6 7	min/maj7	9, 11, 13
Bebop Tonic Minor	1 2 ♭3 4 5 ♯5 6 7	min/maj7	9, 11, 13
Harmonic Minor	1 2 ♭3 4 5 ♭6 7	min/maj7	9, 11
MINOR 7♭5			
Locrian	1 ♭2 ♭3 4 ♭5 ♭6 ♭7	min7♭5	11
Locrian nat9	1 2 ♭3 4 ♭5 ♭6 ♭7	min7♭5	9, 11
Locrian nat6	1 ♭2 ♭3 4 ♭5 6 ♭7	min7♭5	11, 13
DIMINISHED			
Diminished whole/half	1 2 ♭3 4 ♭5 ♯5 6 7	dim7	9, 11, ♯5, maj7

TIPS

1. Know the song's melody

The first thing to do when learning a new song is to learn the melody. It seems like an obvious step, yet sometimes jazz musicians are so eager to get to their solos that they brush off learning the head or treat it as an unnecessary incidental. Knowing a song's melody will also help you keep your place in a song. If you can hear the song's melody going on in your head as you improvise, you will be able to tell where you are in the song's form.

2. Follow the form of a song

If you are new to playing jazz, it's easy to get lost in a tune. When you learn a new tune, it is helpful to first map out the form or structure. Most blues tunes are twelve measures long while most standards are usually thirty-two measures long, or arranged in some multiple of eight measures (sixteen measures, sixty-four measures, etc.). The form of a song can also be labeled alphabetically by section. A typical song structure is a thirty-two-measure AABA, with A representing the first eight-measure phrase and B representing the contrasting section between the first two A sections and the last A section.

3. Listen

If you get lost, stop playing and try to get a sense of where you are. A mistake beginners sometimes make when they get lost is to overplay, "hoping for the best." Most often this compounds the problem. Step back and either try to hear the melody in your head or listen for the rhythm section's clues. If you are really having a hard time, then play whole notes or let several measures go by without playing anything until you know where you are.

4. Stick to chord tones

If a tune has chord changes that are hard to navigate, don't try to play the "hippest" lines or the hardest scales you've been working on just yet. First stick to the basic chord tones (root, 3rd, 5th, or 7th) and focus on "making the changes."

5. Connect to the nearest chord tone in the next chord

The smoothest way to connect chord tones is to move as little as necessary. Figure out if there are common tones between chords. If there are then you could simply just keep using that note across the chord change. If there are no common tones, then find the closest tone in the next chord. There's usually a "right" note not much more than a step away.

6. Think motivically

Rather than thinking of a new scale every time a chord changes, try taking a small fragment and adjusting one or two notes to fit each change.

7. Don't lose your timing

It's very important that you stay rhythmically in tune with the band. This means you have to play along to the same beat as everyone else, whether you are playing whole notes or sixteenth notes. Don't rush or drag your notes. If you feel your time slipping, stop playing and listen for where the beat is.

ALL BLUES

C VERSION

BY MILES DAVIS

DOXY

BY SONNY ROLLINS

CD #1

◆5 : SPLIT TRACK/MELODY
◆6 : FULL STEREO TRACK

C VERSION

AUTUMN LEAVES

CD #1

3 : SPLIT TRACK/MELODY
4 : FULL STEREO TRACK

C VERSION

ENGLISH LYRIC BY JOHNNY MERCER
FRENCH LYRIC BY JACQUES PREVERT
MUSIC BY JOSEPH KOSMA

FOOTPRINTS

C VERSION

BY WAYNE SHORTER

FREDDIE FREELOADER

CD #1

◆9 : SPLIT TRACK/MELODY
◆10 : FULL STEREO TRACK

C VERSION

BY MILES DAVIS

CD #1

C VERSION

HOW INSENSITIVE
(INSENSATEZ)

MUSIC BY ANTONIO CARLOS JOBIM
ORIGINAL WORDS BY VINICIUS DE MORAES
ENGLISH WORDS BY NORMAN GIMBEL

CD #1

: SPLIT TRACK/MELODY

: FULL STEREO TRACK

IMPRESSIONS

BY JOHN COLTRANE

C VERSION

FAST SWING

TO CODA

SOLOS (5 FULL CHORUSES)

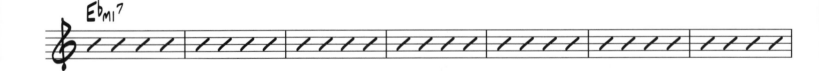

D.C. AL CODA
TAKE REPEAT

CODA

LITTLE SUNFLOWER

CD #1

⬥**15** : SPLIT TRACK/MELODY
⬥**16** : FULL STEREO TRACK

BY FREDDIE HUBBARD

C VERSION

CD #2

◆1 : SPLIT TRACK/MELODY
◆2 : FULL STEREO TRACK

MAIDEN VOYAGE

BY HERBIE HANCOCK

C VERSION

NOW'S THE TIME

BY CHARLIE PARKER

CD #2

3: SPLIT TRACK/MELODY
4: FULL STEREO TRACK

C VERSION

RECORDA-ME

BY JOE HENDERSON

C VERSION

SOLAR

C VERSION

BY MILES DAVIS

SATIN DOLL

BY DUKE ELLINGTON

CD #2

◆7 : SPLIT TRACK/MELODY
◆8 : FULL STEREO TRACK

C VERSION

SONG FOR MY FATHER

C VERSION

WORDS AND MUSIC BY
HORACE SILVER

YESTERDAYS

WORDS BY OTTO HARBACH
MUSIC BY JEROME KERN

C VERSION

ALL BLUES

Bb Version

BY MILES DAVIS

DOXY

BY SONNY ROLLINS

CD #1
◆5 : SPLIT TRACK/MELODY
◆6 : FULL STEREO TRACK

Bb VERSION

AUTUMN LEAVES

ENGLISH LYRIC BY JOHNNY MERCER
FRENCH LYRIC BY JACQUES PRÉVERT
MUSIC BY JOSEPH KOSMA

FOOTPRINTS

Bb VERSION

BY WAYNE SHORTER

CD #1

9 : SPLIT TRACK/MELODY
10 : FULL STEREO TRACK

Bb VERSION

FREDDIE FREELOADER

BY MILES DAVIS

CD #1

⑪ : SPLIT TRACK/MELODY
⑫ : FULL STEREO TRACK

Bb VERSION

HOW INSENSITIVE
(INSENSATEZ)

MUSIC BY ANTONIO CARLOS JOBIM
ORIGINAL WORDS BY VINICIUS DE MORAES
ENGLISH WORDS BY NORMAN GIMBEL

IMPRESSIONS

Bb VERSION

BY JOHN COLTRANE

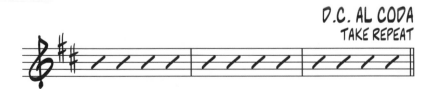

LITTLE SUNFLOWER

BY FREDDIE HUBBARD

CD #2

① : SPLIT TRACK/MELODY
② : FULL STEREO TRACK

MAIDEN VOYAGE

BY HERBIE HANCOCK

Bb VERSION

MEDIUM EVEN 8THS

SOLO (2 CHORUSES)

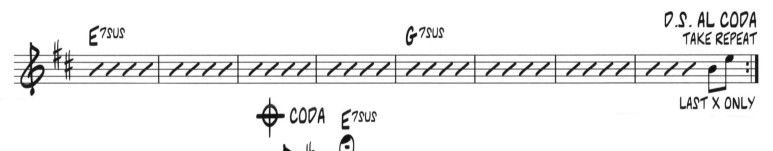

Now's the Time

CD #2
❸ : SPLIT TRACK/MELODY
❹ : FULL STEREO TRACK

BY CHARLIE PARKER

Bb VERSION

RECORDA-ME

BY JOE HENDERSON

Bb VERSION

SOLAR

CD #2

◆ 9 : SPLIT TRACK/MELODY
◆ 10 : FULL STEREO TRACK

Bb VERSION

BY MILES DAVIS

SATIN DOLL

CD #2
- 7 : SPLIT TRACK/MELODY
- 8 : FULL STEREO TRACK

BY Duke Ellington

Bb VERSION

11 : SPLIT TRACK/MELODY
12 : FULL STEREO TRACK

SONG FOR MY FATHER

Bb VERSION

WORDS AND MUSIC BY
HORACE SILVER

YESTERDAYS

CD #2

◆13 : SPLIT TRACK/MELODY
◆14 : FULL STEREO TRACK

WORDS BY OTTO HARBACH
MUSIC BY JEROME KERN

Bb VERSION

ALL BLUES

Eb VERSION

BY MILES DAVIS

DOXY

BY SONNY ROLLINS

CD #1
- ◆ 5 : SPLIT TRACK/MELODY
- ◆ 6 : FULL STEREO TRACK

Eb VERSION

AUTUMN LEAVES

CD #1
3 : SPLIT TRACK/MELODY
4 : FULL STEREO TRACK

Eb VERSION

ENGLISH LYRIC BY JOHNNY MERCER
FRENCH LYRIC BY JACQUES PREVERT
MUSIC BY JOSEPH KOSMA

CD #1

◆ 7 : SPLIT TRACK/MELODY
◆ 8 : FULL STEREO TRACK

FOOTPRINTS

Eb VERSION

BY WAYNE SHORTER

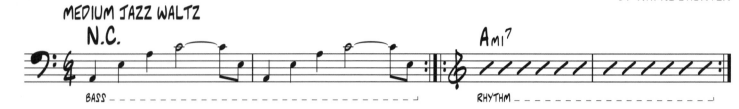

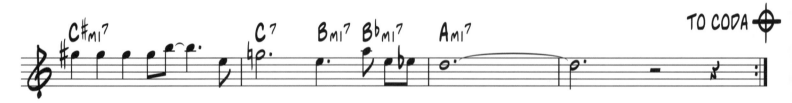

SOLOS (5 CHORUSES)

CD #1

9: SPLIT TRACK/MELODY
10: FULL STEREO TRACK

Eb VERSION

FREDDIE FREELOADER

BY MILES DAVIS

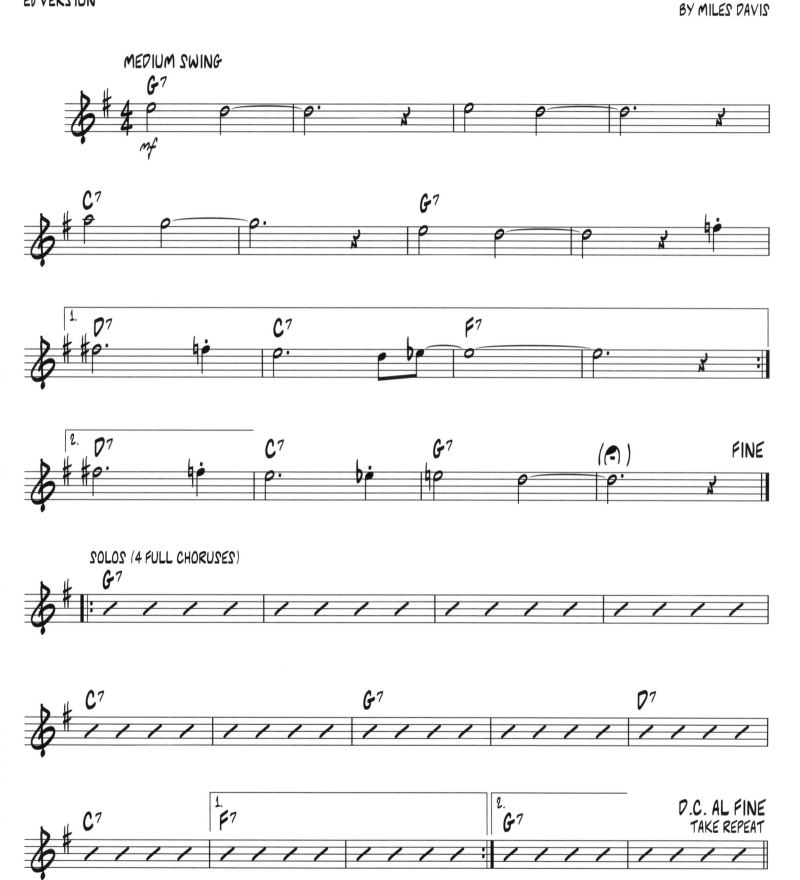

CD #1

◆11 : SPLIT TRACK/MELODY
◆12 : FULL STEREO TRACK

Eb VERSION

HOW INSENSITIVE
(INSENSATEZ)

MUSIC BY ANTONIO CARLOS JOBIM
ORIGINAL WORDS BY VINICIUS DE MORAES
ENGLISH WORDS BY NORMAN GIMBEL

CD #1

13 : SPLIT TRACK/MELODY
14 : FULL STEREO TRACK

IMPRESSIONS

Eb VERSION

BY JOHN COLTRANE

CD #1
15 : SPLIT TRACK/MELODY
16 : FULL STEREO TRACK

LITTLE SUNFLOWER

BY FREDDIE HUBBARD

Eb VERSION

CD #2
1: SPLIT TRACK/MELODY
2: FULL STEREO TRACK

MAIDEN VOYAGE

BY HERBIE HANCOCK

Eb VERSION

NOW'S THE TIME

BY CHARLIE PARKER

Eb VERSION

RECORDA-ME

BY JOE HENDERSON

Eb VERSION

SOLAR

SATIN DOLL

BY DUKE ELLINGTON

11 : SPLIT TRACK/MELODY
12 : FULL STEREO TRACK

SONG FOR MY FATHER

WORDS AND MUSIC BY
HORACE SILVER

Eb VERSION

Yesterdays

13 : SPLIT TRACK/MELODY
14 : FULL STEREO TRACK

WORDS BY OTTO HARBACH
MUSIC BY JEROME KERN

Eb VERSION

ALL BLUES

CD #1
1: SPLIT TRACK/MELODY
2: FULL STEREO TRACK

BY MILES DAVIS

DOXY

CD #1

5: SPLIT TRACK/MELODY
6: FULL STEREO TRACK

C VERSION

BY SONNY ROLLINS

AUTUMN LEAVES

ENGLISH LYRIC BY JOHNNY MERCER
FRENCH LYRIC BY JACQUES PREVERT
MUSIC BY JOSEPH KOSMA

FOOTPRINTS

BY WAYNE SHORTER

FREDDIE FREELOADER

CD #1

◆9 : SPLIT TRACK/MELODY

◆10 : FULL STEREO TRACK

𝄢 : C VERSION

BY MILES DAVIS

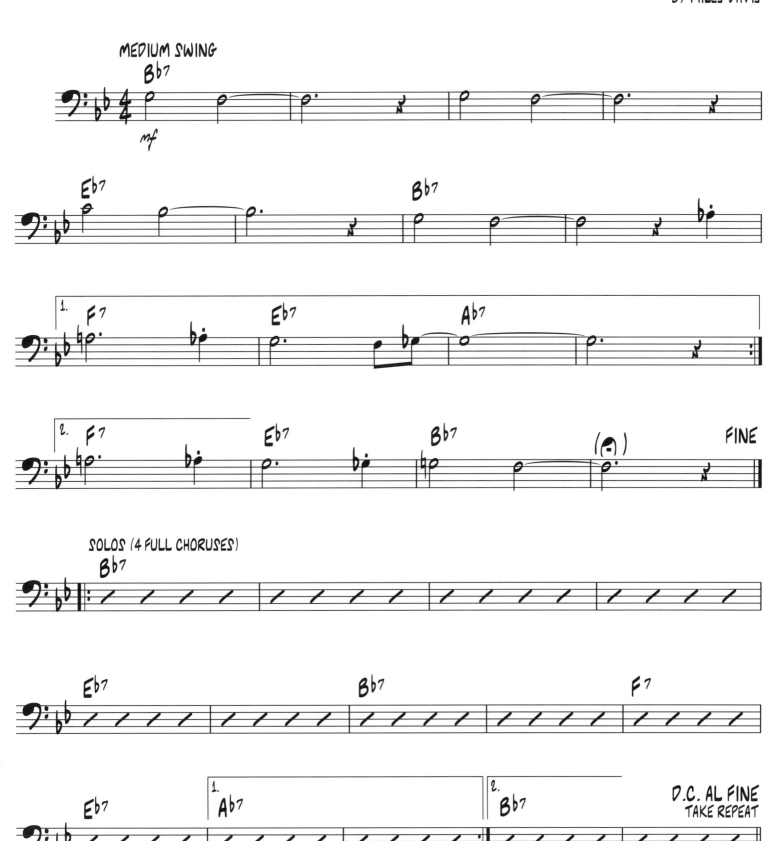

CD #1

11 : SPLIT TRACK/MELODY
12 : FULL STEREO TRACK

𝄢: C VERSION

HOW INSENSITIVE
(INSENSATEZ)

MUSIC BY ANTONIO CARLOS JOBIM
ORIGINAL WORDS BY VINICIUS DE MORAES
ENGLISH WORDS BY NORMAN GIMBEL

CD #1

13 : SPLIT TRACK/MELODY
14 : FULL STEREO TRACK

𝄢 C VERSION

IMPRESSIONS

BY JOHN COLTRANE

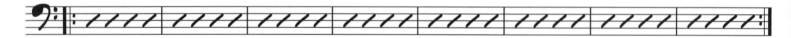

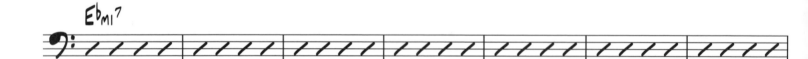

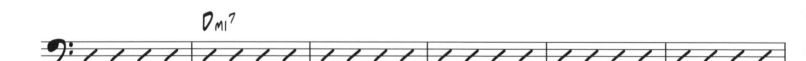

LITTLE SUNFLOWER

BY FREDDIE HUBBARD

CD #1
- 15 : SPLIT TRACK/MELODY
- 16 : FULL STEREO TRACK

𝄢: C VERSION

MAIDEN VOYAGE

BY HERBIE HANCOCK

NOW'S THE TIME

BY CHARLIE PARKER

𝄢: C VERSION

RECORDA-ME

BY JOE HENDERSON

CD #2

⑤ : SPLIT TRACK/MELODY
⑥ : FULL STEREO TRACK

𝄢 : C VERSION

SOLAR

BY MILES DAVIS

CD #2

◆ 9 : SPLIT TRACK/MELODY
◆ 10 : FULL STEREO TRACK

𝄢: C VERSION

CD #2

◆ 7 : SPLIT TRACK/MELODY
◆ 8 : FULL STEREO TRACK

SATIN DOLL

BY DUKE ELLINGTON

𝄢: C VERSION

CD #2

11 : SPLIT TRACK/MELODY
12 : FULL STEREO TRACK

𝄢 C VERSION

SONG FOR MY FATHER

WORDS AND MUSIC BY
HORACE SILVER

Yesterdays

WORDS BY OTTO HARBACH
MUSIC BY JEROME KERN

CD #2
13 : SPLIT TRACK/MELODY
14 : FULL STEREO TRACK

Presenting the Hal Leonard JAZZ PLAY-ALONG SERIES

1. DUKE ELLINGTON
00841644 ....$16.95

2. MILES DAVIS
00841645 ....$16.95

3. THE BLUES
00841646 ....$16.99

4. JAZZ BALLADS
00841691 ....$16.99

5. BEST OF BEBOP
00841689 ....$16.99

6. JAZZ CLASSICS WITH EASY CHANGES
00841690 ....$16.99

7. ESSENTIAL JAZZ STANDARDS
00843000 ....$16.99

8. ANTONIO CARLOS JOBIM AND THE ART OF THE BOSSA NOVA
00843001 ....$16.95

9. DIZZY GILLESPIE
00843002 ....$16.99

10. DISNEY CLASSICS
00843003 ....$16.99

11. RODGERS AND HART – FAVORITES
00843004 ....$16.99

12. ESSENTIAL JAZZ CLASSICS
00843005 ....$16.99

13. JOHN COLTRANE
00843006 ....$16.95

14. IRVING BERLIN
00843007 ....$15.99

15. RODGERS & HAMMERSTEIN
00843008 ....$15.99

16. COLE PORTER
00843009 ....$15.95

17. COUNT BASIE
00843010 ....$16.95

18. HAROLD ARLEN
00843011 ....$15.95

19. COOL JAZZ
00843012 ....$15.95

20. CHRISTMAS CAROLS
00843080 ....$14.95

21. RODGERS AND HART – CLASSICS
00843014 ....$14.95

22. WAYNE SHORTER
00843015 ....$16.95

23. LATIN JAZZ
00843016 ....$16.95

24. EARLY JAZZ STANDARDS
00843017 ....$14.95

25. CHRISTMAS JAZZ
00843018 ....$16.95

26. CHARLIE PARKER
00843019 ....$16.95

27. GREAT JAZZ STANDARDS
00843020 ....$15.99

28. BIG BAND ERA
00843021 ....$15.99

29. LENNON AND McCARTNEY
00843022 ....$16.95

30. BLUES' BEST
00843023 ....$15.99

31. JAZZ IN THREE
00843024 ....$15.99

32. BEST OF SWING
00843025 ....$15.99

33. SONNY ROLLINS
00843029 ....$15.95

34. ALL TIME STANDARDS
00843030 ....$15.99

35. BLUESY JAZZ
00843031 ....$15.99

36. HORACE SILVER
00843032 ....$16.99

37. BILL EVANS
00843033 ....$16.95

38. YULETIDE JAZZ
00843034 ....$16.95

39. "ALL THE THINGS YOU ARE" & MORE JEROME KERN SONGS
00843035 ....$15.99

40. BOSSA NOVA
00843036 ....$15.99

41. CLASSIC DUKE ELLINGTON
00843037 ....$16.99

42. GERRY MULLIGAN – FAVORITES
00843038 ....$16.99

43. GERRY MULLIGAN – CLASSICS
00843039 ....$16.95

44. OLIVER NELSON
00843040 ....$16.95

45. JAZZ AT THE MOVIES
00843041 ....$15.99

46. BROADWAY JAZZ STANDARDS
00843042 ....$15.99

47. CLASSIC JAZZ BALLADS
00843043 ....$15.99

48. BEBOP CLASSICS
00843044 ....$16.99

49. MILES DAVIS – STANDARDS
00843045 ....$16.95

50. GREAT JAZZ CLASSICS
00843046 ....$15.99

51. UP-TEMPO JAZZ
00843047 ....$15.99

52. STEVIE WONDER
00843048 ....$15.95

53. RHYTHM CHANGES
00843049 ....$15.99

54. "MOONLIGHT IN VERMONT" & OTHER GREAT STANDARDS
00843050 ....$15.99

55. BENNY GOLSON
00843052 ....$15.95

56. "GEORGIA ON MY MIND" & OTHER SONGS BY HOAGY CARMICHAEL
00843056 ....$15.99

57. VINCE GUARALDI
00843057 ....$16.99

58. MORE LENNON AND McCARTNEY
00843059 ....$15.99

59. SOUL JAZZ
00843060 ....$15.99

60. DEXTER GORDON
00843061 ....$15.95

61. MONGO SANTAMARIA
00843062 ....$15.95

62. JAZZ-ROCK FUSION
00843063 ....$14.95

63. CLASSICAL JAZZ
00843064 ....$14.95

64. TV TUNES
00843065 ....$14.95

65. SMOOTH JAZZ
00843066 ....$16.99

66. A CHARLIE BROWN CHRISTMAS
00843067 ....$16.99

67. CHICK COREA
00843068 ....$15.95

68. CHARLES MINGUS
00843069 ....$16.95

69. CLASSIC JAZZ
00843071 ....$15.99

70. THE DOORS
00843072 ....$14.95

71. COLE PORTER CLASSICS
00843073 ....$14.95

72. CLASSIC JAZZ BALLADS
00843074 ....$15.99

73. JAZZ/BLUES
00843075 ....$14.95

74. BEST JAZZ CLASSICS
00843076 ....$15.99

75. PAUL DESMOND
00843077 ....$14.95

76. BROADWAY JAZZ BALLADS
00843078 ....$15.99

77. JAZZ ON BROADWAY
00843079 ....$15.99

78. STEELY DAN
00843070 ....$14.99

79. MILES DAVIS – CLASSICS
00843081 ....$15.99

80. JIMI HENDRIX
00843083 ....$15.99

81. FRANK SINATRA – CLASSICS
00843084 ....$15.99

82. FRANK SINATRA – STANDARDS
00843085 ....$15.99

83. ANDREW LLOYD WEBBER
00843104 ....$14.95

84. BOSSA NOVA CLASSICS
00843105 ....$14.95

85. MOTOWN HITS
00843109 ....$14.95

86. BENNY GOODMAN
00843110 ....$14.95

87. DIXIELAND
00843111 ....$14.95

88. DUKE ELLINGTON FAVORITES
00843112 ....$14.95

89. IRVING BERLIN FAVORITES
00843113 ....$14.95

90. THELONIOUS MONK CLASSICS
00841262 ....$16.99

91. THELONIOUS MONK FAVORITES
00841263 ....$16.99

92. LEONARD BERNSTEIN
00450134 ....$14.99

93. DISNEY FAVORITES
00843142 ....$14.99

94. RAY
00843143 ....$14.95

95. JAZZ AT THE LOUNGE
00843144 ....$14.99

96. LATIN JAZZ STANDARDS
00843145 ....$14.99

97. MAYBE I'M AMAZED
00843148 ....$14.99

98. DAVE FRISHBERG
00843149 ....$15.99

99. SWINGING STANDARDS
00843150 ....$14.99

100. LOUIS ARMSTRONG
00740423 ....$15.99

101. BUD POWELL
00843152 ....$14.99

102. JAZZ POP
00843153 ....$14.99

103. ON GREEN DOLPHIN STREET & OTHER JAZZ CLASSICS
00843154 ....$14.99

104. ELTON JOHN
00843155 ....$14.99

105. SOULFUL JAZZ
00843151 ....$14.99

106. SLO' JAZZ
00843117 ....$14.99

107. MOTOWN CLASSICS
00843116 ....$14.99

111. COOL CHRISTMAS
00843162 ....$15.99

For use with all B-flat, E-flat, Bass Clef and C instruments, the Jazz Play-Along® Series is the ultimate learning tool for all jazz musicians. With musician-friendly lead sheets, melody cues, and other split-track choices on the included CD, these first-of-a-kind packages help you master improvisation while playing some of the greatest tunes of all time. FOR STUDY, each tune includes a split track with: melody cue with proper style and inflection • professional rhythm tracks • choruses for soloing • removable bass part • removable piano part. FOR PERFORMANCE, each tune also has: an additional full stereo accompaniment track (no melody) • additional choruses for soloing.

Prices, contents, and availability subject to change without notice.

FOR MORE INFORMATION, SEE YOUR LOCAL MUSIC DEALER, OR WRITE TO:

HAL•LEONARD® CORPORATION
7777 W. BLUEMOUND RD. P.O. BOX 13819
MILWAUKEE, WISCONSIN 53213

Visit Hal Leonard online at
www.halleonard.com
for complete songlists.

0809